I dedicate this book to the many fallen souls in urban America. May their families find peace in the shadows of grief; May they rest peacefully. To my family for always supporting me, I say thank you and I love you all. I also want to thank the city of Baltimore, for providing me with interesting experiences that heavily impacted my life.

Junist Harvey Jr.

"for Baltimore"

GRASS ROOTS POETRY

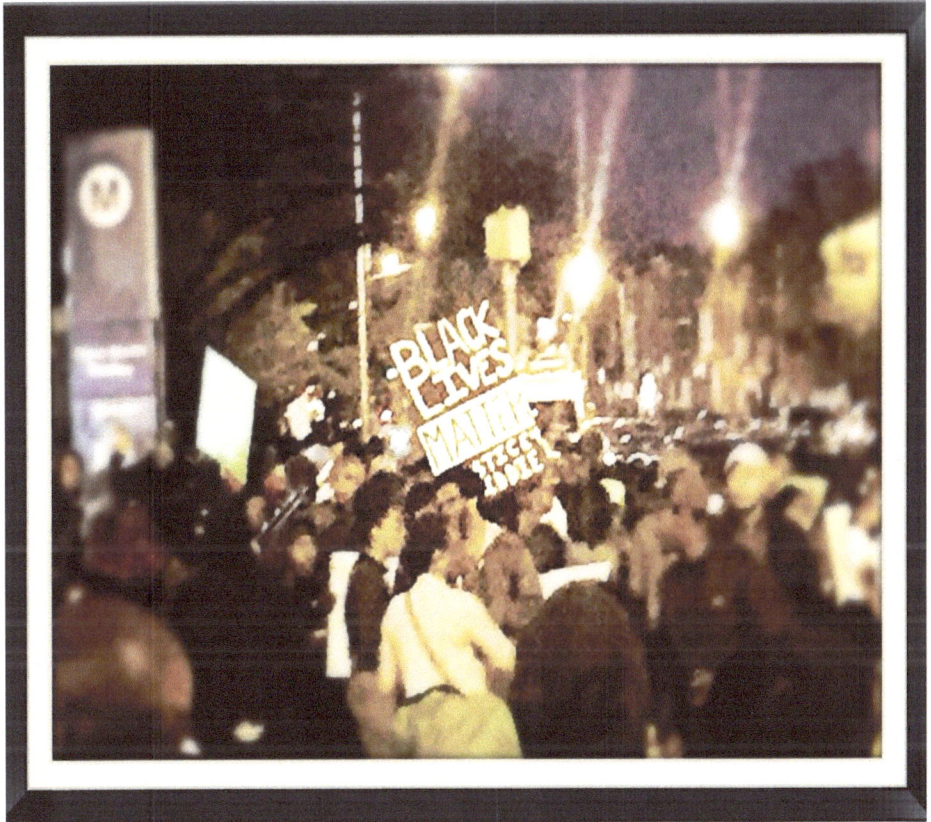

Junist Harvey Jr.

PREFACE

With the recent unrest in the city of Baltimore, Maryland, many discussions have been centered on poverty, crime, and the many other hardships of inner city living.Though many may offer several different opinions, most fail to examine the true causes of the demise of urban living across the nation. As we usher in the age of gentrification and hipsters in Harlem, we must examine why these spaces that were once considered abysmal, are now the bastions of prosperity and upward mobility. No true discussion can be had unless we examine the entire situation, which is vast in its implications. No true discussion can be had unless the entire system which created the slums in urban America is examined critically. An understanding of redlining, lead paint poisoning, the War on Drugs, and the political spectrum will lead the next wave of solution based analysis.

Growing up in the 90's and 2000's in Baltimore, it was evident that a lot of people were going in and out of prison. To add insult to injury, many people who wereout of prison were addicted to crack cocaine or heroin. "President Ronald Reagan officially announces the current drug war in 1982, before crack became an issue in the media or a crisis in poor black neighborhoods." (Alexander, 2012) During that era, the United States prison population rose from three hundred thousand to two million. A significant rise in the prison population, coupled with the fact that a war was declared on crack cocaine prior to its arrival in urban America, proves certain conspiracies surrounding urban demise to be true. When a government has no plan of rehabilitation for the people they arrest, recidivism is the only outcome one can expect. It is absolutely absurd to expect someone to blend into society after doing hard time in a penal institution without proper rehabilitation. The War on Drugs kept families separated, whether by bars, or the burden of drug addiction. "The budget of the National Institute on Drug Abuse wasreduced from two hundred seventy four million dollars to fifty seven million dollars from 1981 to 1984, and antidrug funds allocated to the Department of Education were cut from fourteen million dollars to three million dollars." (Alexander, 2012)

The impact of political giddiness created a community of people who would legally face discrimination for the rest of their lives. A community asked to pull itself up by its own boot straps, is becoming aware that outside influences played a large role in the unpleasant circumstances we now find in urban America.

How did the ghettos of urban America become a reality? The new liberals of today will have you to believe it's a question of economics, when in reality, the ghettos of urban America were deliberately created. Redlining was common in cities like Baltimore, Detroit, Philadelphia, etc. Redlining is defined as the drawing of redlines on neighborhood maps signaling which neighborhoods would be denied mortgage loans. In those redlined areas, families were forced into contract home sales. "One of the most pernicious was the practice of 'contract' home sales, in which black homebuyers were essentially roped into buying their property 'on time,' the way you might a television or dishwasher: making payments (at inflated rates of interest), until the entire 'loan' (far larger than the actual value of the house) had been paid off. Even one late payment would typically cause the borrower to be considered in default, and the holder of the contract would then take the property back from the borrower, reselling it to some other unlucky customer." (Wise, 2015). White flight of the mid 1900's, in essence, created the ghettos that still exist today. When the white residents left neighborhoods like Edmondson Village in Baltimore; new neighborhoods were created in suburbia for those who chose to leave. Black residents were met with "for sale" signs from their new white neighbors upon arrival. The fear created by speculators, (who would convince a white resident to sell his/her home before "The Blacks" came) created the segregated communities of today. As the white residents abandoned these neighborhoods, so did the local government, and later businesses. "And then there's Martin O'Malley, the Democratic former governor with presidential aspirations. When he was mayor of Baltimore, O'Malley also criticized the settlement- in effect, a judicially mandated MTO project that required the U.S. Department of Housing and Urban Development to stop segregating poor black families in decrepit inner-city public housing projects and allow them to move." (Rodrickks, 2015).

It's almost taboo to discuss the ills of urban America as done in the previous paragraphs. The topic of urban demise is usually dominated by the conservative right, with images of black woman on welfare and food stamps. Though the true cause of urban demise is multifaceted, somehow the false narratives of lack of personal responsibility continue to dominate. The purpose of Grass Roots Poetry is to generate dialogue around the issues that plague every community in urban America.

Junist Harvey Jr.

TABLE OF CONTENTS

Sunrise

HighNoon

PART 2

Sunset

Sunrise

"Maybe the values of death outweigh the value of life "

Untitled

Babies become kids, who become adults
Getting older with the world at no one's fault
Minds cultivate as wide eyed youth replace adults

Natural displacement, impatient youth become adults
Just as impatient as the world, who wants to assault them whole
Dying from poverty instead of old age
Who shot at me, becomes the new saying

Too young to realize what potential lingers on to their lives
Nothing but social media posts, as a result when he dies
Flowers and balloons on the sidewalk where he lied

Another lifeless soul placed back in the hanger of lives lost
No value can explain how much these lives cost
Just tossed away and lost forever

Maybe they're well off or better   yet
Maybe the values of death outweigh the values of life
I question that

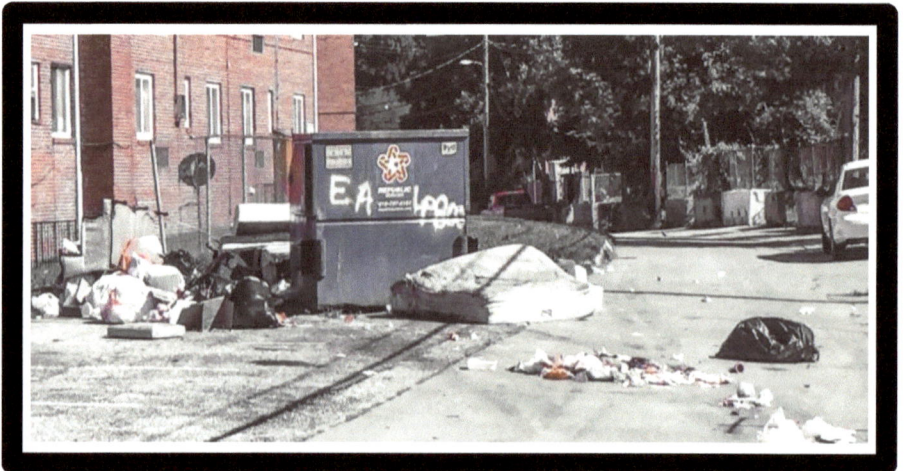

Mr. Garner

Eric garnered the attention of the world in a fight for his life
A fight that forced him to the light, far before his detriment was in sight
His crime is up for dispute
But whether they produce evidence of selling untaxed cigarettes
I question the consequence of death
The misuse of loose cigarettes is not a fair trade for a man's life
As if his mere existence was Panteleo's decision
His grip tightened in response to dying cries
Convincing himself of how he tried resisting
Enjoying the moment, fueling an adrenaline addiction
Untaxed tobacco, in exchange for trachea constriction
Twisted fear and xenophobic conviction
Exudes patriotism to the privileged citizen
Why police a community if you're afraid of the people who live in it

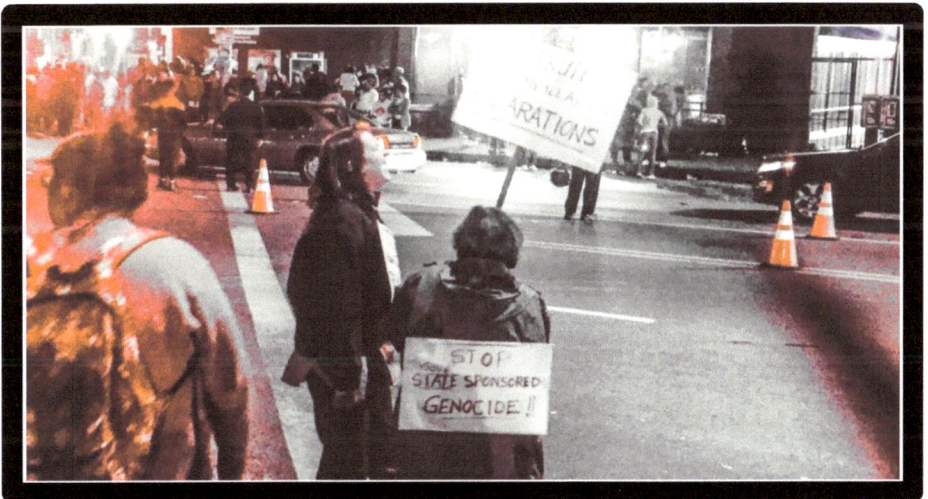

Resuscitate

Return yourself to your soul
As if outside influences are no longer gold
You are your own judge; your shell is your robe
Your sword and gable is your brain exposed
Your thoughts matter, believe it
Be powerful
Expose ignorance when you see it
Revive yourself to know yourself
Grow more each day and show yourself your worth
Find out what debt is owed for your w o r k
Pay it to your health and refresh your organs like birth

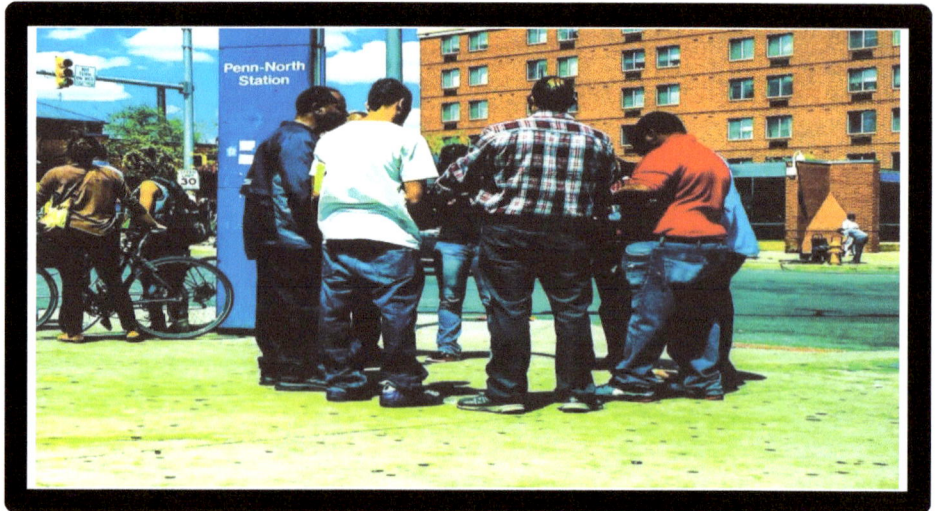

My Hair

My hair can shape shift and make this head a mantel for a masterpiece
My hair can change texture with the seasons
Giving reason to why some call me nappy
Sure my hair tangles
But it's not mangled
Though it may make some unhappy
No my afro won't have folks clapping
But I'm asking that my hair not be a deciding factor
For employment, or a fraternal chapter
Or opportunity to be a master
Should I decide to grow dred locks
Don't dead lock me out of lasting happiness
Don't rationalize your quotations of uniformity and conformity
How I appear to the naked eye is only a part of me
The outer shell is only a cover for the heart of me
Instead of being judgmental of what's above my mental shell
Be critical of your mentality as well

Why Did You Kill Him?

Why did you kill him?
Were you unaware of the clock that stops after bussing your glock
Did you know you would end a life with one strike of your pocket knife

Are you that desensitized to life ending, that you smile at the thought
Never mind offending his wife his children
And the woman who gave him his beginning

Your grinning sends chills through society
Not to mention your utter happiness sending chills through the family
They want you to suffer
As you force them to recover from your sudden destruction

You must've believed there was nothing he could offer the world
Or were you unaware of murder's international consequences
The pearl you stole was the cornerstone of well intention

No he wasn't awarded honorable mentions
Nor given pendants for services rendered
But who are you to decide when his life is to be finished

DAVID A. McLAUGHLIN, JR.
JAN. 13, 1987 — MAR. 20, 2011
LOVING FATHER, BROTHER, SON, FRIEND
LIFE IS MY STRUGGLE

The Cool

The cool is real but, how physical is it
Can you touch or feel its presence
Or listen to it

Can it be defined
Or can examples be listed
Is it embodied by the gifted
Or can the average Joe be equipped with it

How does it manifest when shifted into culture
Is it allowed in the office
Can it be placed on a poster
How much of it shall I shoulder
Or must it be filed away in a folder
I suppose cool has no odor,
Or is my sense of smell too mediocre

Can cool be too rare to detect with bifocals
Or are we chasing our imagination
Becoming complacent, losing focus

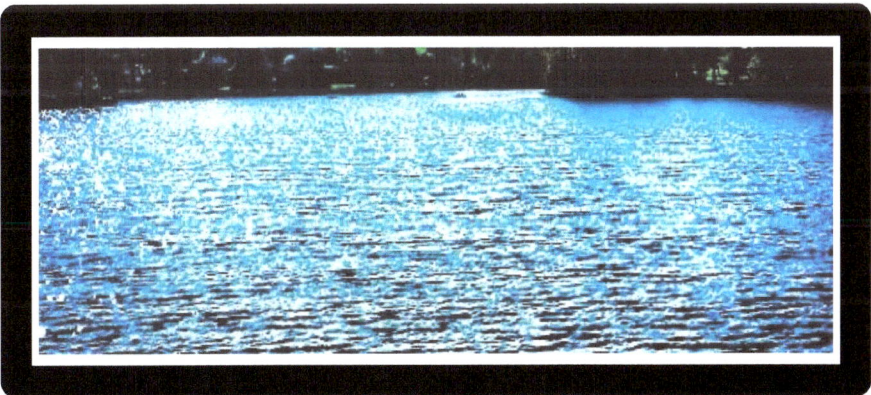

Letter to the Mayor

We've prayed for fairer conditions
Jobs which provide an honest living
And forgiving for debts paid to society
For a past that's not left privy

Mrs. Mayor what's next for this city
Gentrification just seems like shitty business
Are you willing to resist it
Or are you willing to sacrifice our existence
Although crime and murder will do it anyway without assistance

Is it your preference that we don't survive
I ask that while wondering your prize for this continuance of crime
I wonder if you're in line with politicians who lie
Or will you stand and fight the good fight or at least try

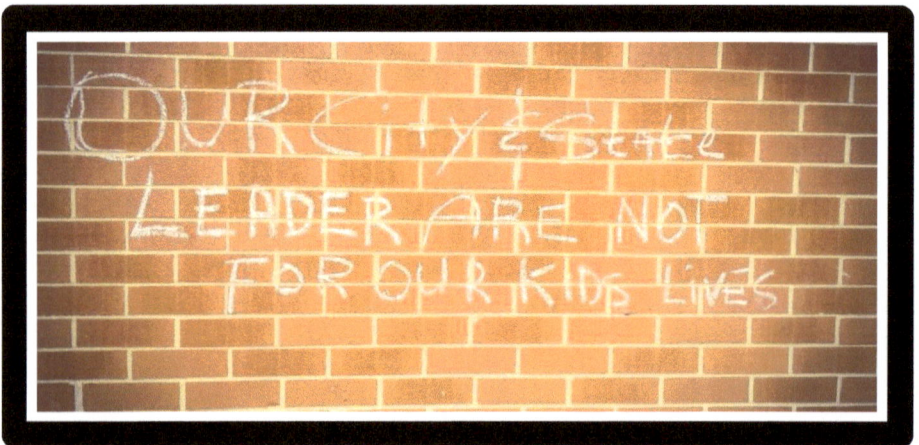

Some Spare Change

On a gorgeous day
I choose to play in traffic for hours on in
I choose to pace that sidewalk, the center island
Asking for spare change or a dollar even
Hoping I could buy a sandwich when I'm leaving
I have no home nor food to eat
I have neither clothes nor bed to sleep
I am unemployed but I haven't given up
Hopefully some spare change can add some better luck
But what I'm hoping for is empathy
I hope those that drive by see a soul inside of me
Sure, I too was productive in society
But I stumbled somewhere I probably shouldn't have
Went downhill fast, but I'm proud that I didn't crash

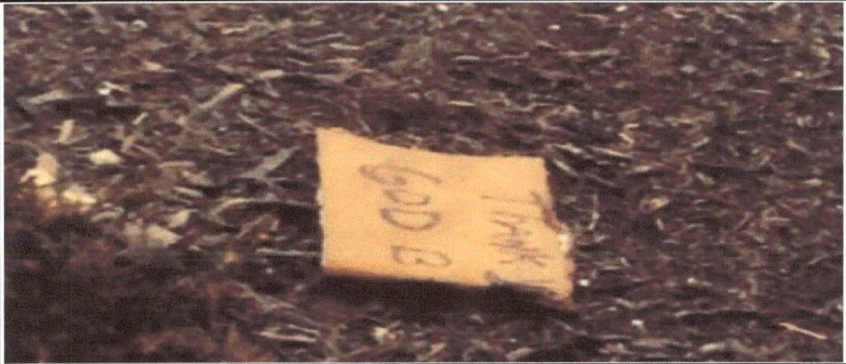

Nothing Extra

I've carried the weight of a nation while raising a family.
I've worked for free while others lived lavishly
Material possessions they attach to me
Desperate times
But desperate measures were no match for me
Wish I could relax on a beach
Take a vacation
But that's out of reach with the rate of inflation
How can I be patient on this 40 hour rotation
When retirement is the only end to this plantation

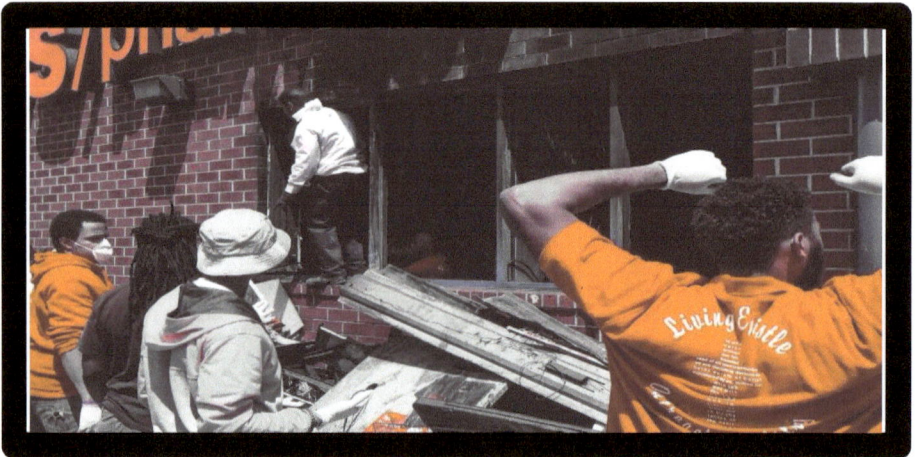

Miracle

Bonding for life is real
Love and passion made a deal
Sealed for eternity
Digested like a meal
Love u can feel and touch
Squeeze and clutch
Trust in love, neglect for lust
As the tear drops crust
Two souls return to peace
What once made you cry, now allows a smile to breath
A piece of me, is a piece of she
She returns a piece back to me
As we become one
We've created a new soul
A daughter or son

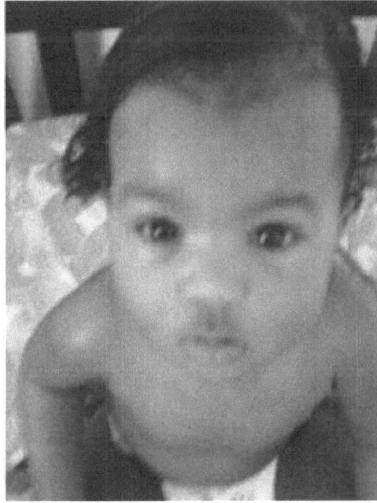

I Am

I am love and I know it
I will no longer clog my thought beltway with negativity
Causing jams and crashes
Killing the soul of the land traveler

I am pain and I know it
I will no longer mask the hurt or distract the pain receptors
Excepting the collective opinion, instead of going in my own direction

I am strong and I know it
I carry a shoulder of weight like a boulder
Posting my pain on networks of social media, bleeding me emotionally

I am focused and I know it
Eye on the prize, a sight never lost
Seen from miles
Goals to be reached, seen from a distance
With vision like an owl

When Will It Change

When will it change
When will we change
Will we change
Or will things remain the same

Some hate life
To the point that some take life
For granted or out of this world

A pearl stolen
Robbed in broad day light
Red blood stains on the concrete, still fresh
While police captains take advantage of the media and press

Never shall we lessen the value of life
And value the lifeless
Whether it be souls trapped in the pipeline to prison stress
Or souls gone on to a place beyond vision
Show them the way while they still have their ears to listen

HighNoon

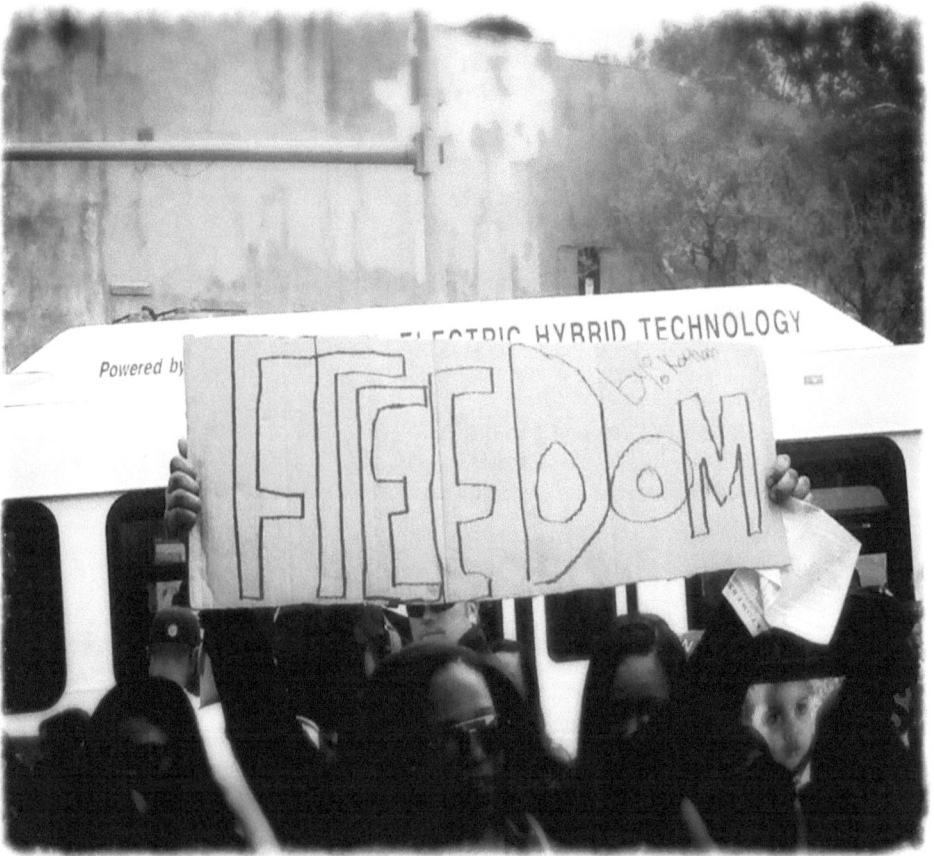

"No I will not be afraid, the power of fear no longer
weighs me down"

Millennial Baby-Boomer

We came in mass
Our numbers outnumber those from the past
Our influence is far reaching even though very few are teaching
Who's keeping the fearless generation from reaping the benefits of their elders
Who's keeping them divided and separated in theory
Who's overcrowding their communities, keeping them weary
Clearly there are issues within, but who's suppressing the loudest voice of reason
While old folks long for the good ole dayz and seasons
The young millennial changes the world and regards anything otherwise as treason

#NoFilter

The body is born nude without cover
No clothing, no other materials to hide your flaws
No beauty standards
No beauty laws
No make up to take off
No superficial men to show off for
With nothing to offer you
No more disrespect as they call for you
From a distance; where listening, only a dog would do
He bothers you, for what his eyes can see
What lies beneath the epidermis
He's not concerned with
While yearning for your approval
He degrades you

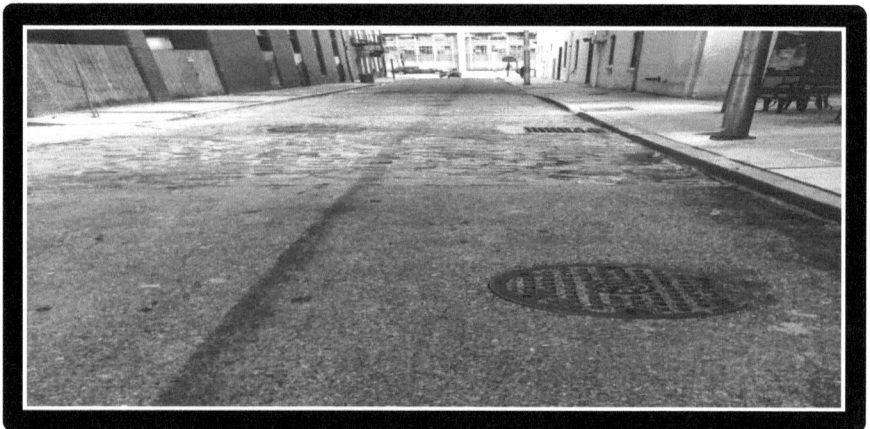

Do Unto...

Morality usually begets no casualty
Some casually disregard conventionality
Morality always overrides ideology
At least it should in any democracy
Forced hypocrisy, now society resembles atrocities
Vacant houses and lots sold to the highest investor
Or owned by the city and left to rot
The rest of us just play catch-up
While politicians dress up and play thespian
The mess we're in expands and never lessens
Reducing classroom lessons is their only solution I'm guessing
Memorization for standardized testing, neglecting critical thinking
Why would these kids want to board a ship that's already sinking

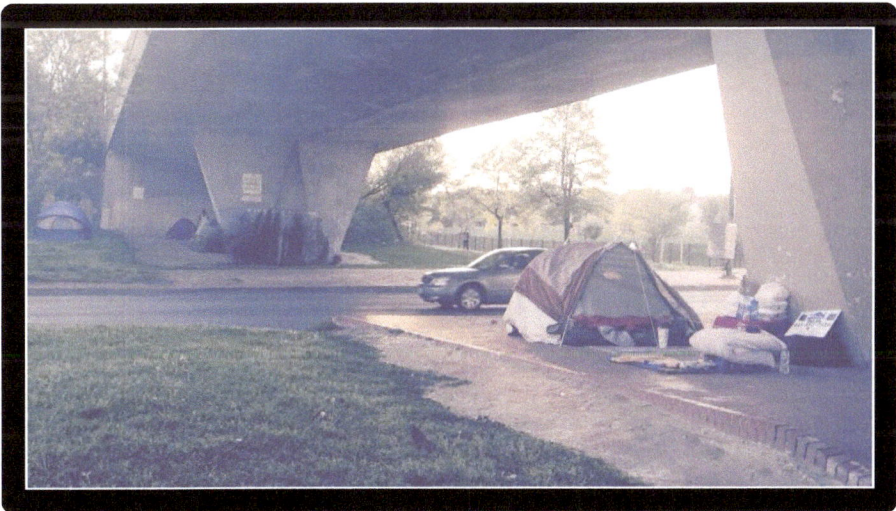

Fearless

No I will not be afraid
The power of fear no longer weighs me down
For fear is no more mountain I climb
It no longer exists in my eye or beneath my chest
I watched fear die a slow but powerful death
Just stood there at rest as fear took its last breath
Fear shall not force me to tear
Its mere presence I shall not lend an ear
Nor shall I hear its pessimism
Anxiety won't consume me entirely
Nor will criticism retire me

Untitled

Sleep was never a thought
To lie down and close my eyes
Never crossed my mind
My body would just shut down in time
Often without even a sign
But my spirit is now aware of rest
Sometimes my body won't shut down for 8 hrs at best
My temple is tired
My mind can attest
Why so hard to recharge
Why must I wait to Hibernate and drift away

City Block

The concrete is un-even
Pac convinced me
Had me believing a rose could sprout
From a crack in the cement
Not the weeds that I'm used to seeing
But a flower could sprout during the sunny season
Soon to be eaten or destroyed for no reason
Showing how cruel nature can be in its natural state of being
It thrives, though unseasoned
Its life is cut short
No longer living
No longer breathing

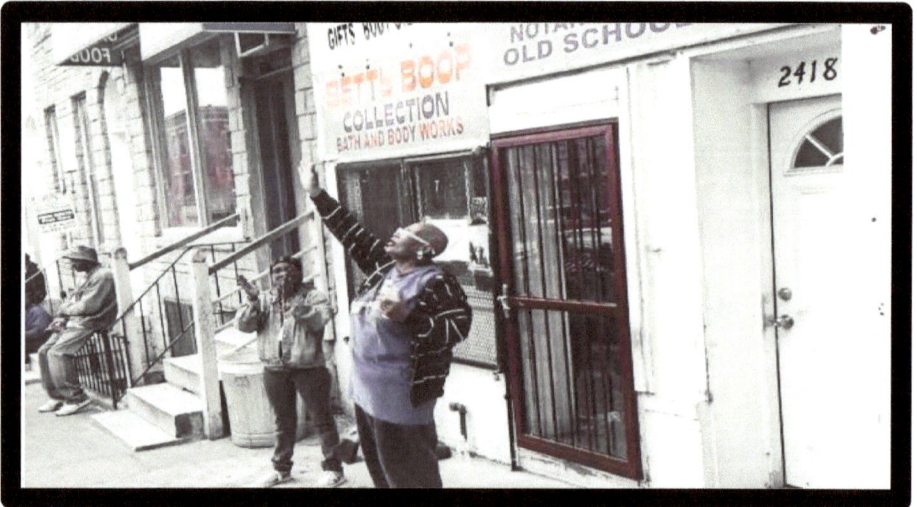

Conflict

Situations arise and alter our thinking
Placing blame and praise on a side without even blinking
Controlling our everyday lives and linking our past experiences
While fearing our peers who we don't take seriously
Clearly there are differences amongst us all
But our differences should not be the reason one falls off

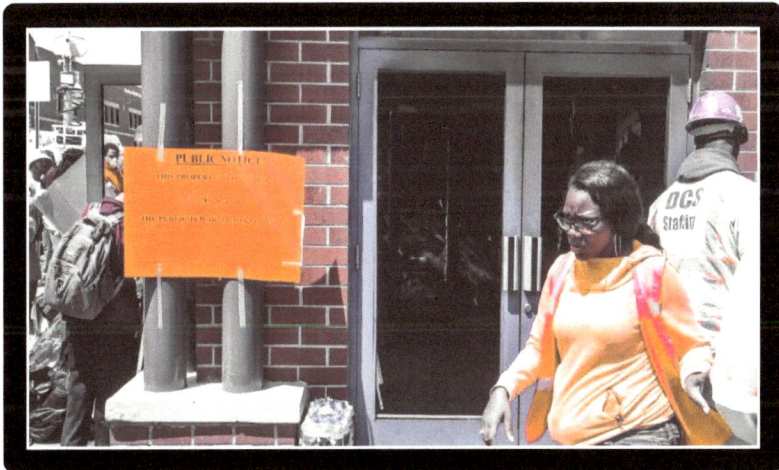

Grow

Maturity is nature's cure
As we age, our view becomes bird's eye
Each decision forces one to analyze
Retract statements and apologize
How can pride determine a man's size
When the heart is the center of his life
Yet pride consumes us like a pipe addiction
Kicking us in the ass to submission

Burn

It burned like the feeling of unfed tummies
Hunger is fire in your gut
But money is where funny politics focus
Hope is all that's left for those in   motion
Until they lash out because they've been silenced on purpose
Voices that should be heard
Conversations and ideas should be put in word
Instead of in pharmacies that burned
Do you hear the cry from the unwanted
Can you feel the presence of the undaunted

Sunset

Part 3

"Why do you shoot when you see brown; although no weapons are ever found"

Cops 'N' Robbers

What's your motive for policing areas where u wouldn't be a homeowner
Who asked you to occupy our tribal sides of town
Why do you shoot when you see brown although no weapons are ever found
Why do you seek excitement in policing the poor
While boredom causes you to create a situation
Where you are frightened even more
What's your issue, or did you realize your misuse of authority
We know your overseer mentality
It's your reality of police work
Can we at least work together
Instead of playing cops 'N' robbers
How about you try to make our lives better

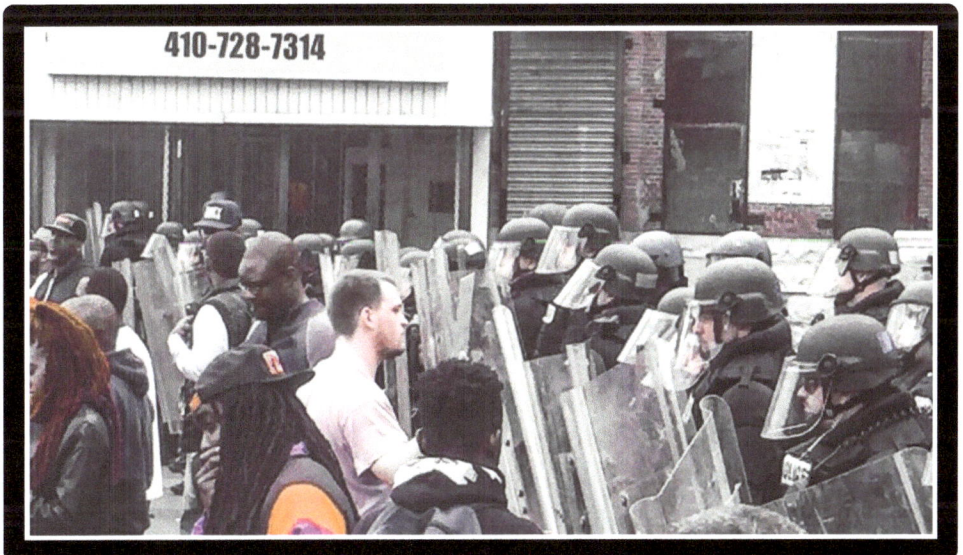

Change

In due time, some change
Sometime, time is change
Time is currency which makes change
Change becomes life because life never stays the same
Make the necessary change before it makes you
You decide change or it will decide you
Change is new and sometimes uncouth
It's the only constant, which remains true
Fools never change
Same baggage that ravaged becomes them like a name
Same pain just hangs
Always on the brain
No longer sane
Looking elsewhere for blame

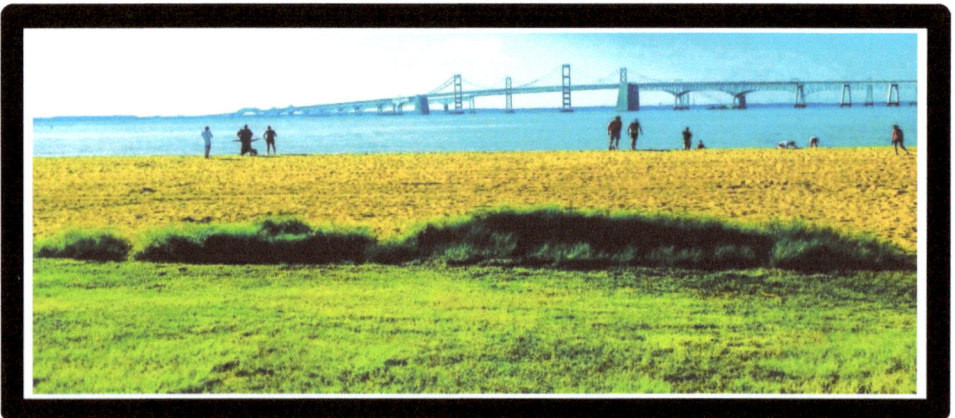

Keep Moving

When the going gets tough
I just keep going
Keep floating like a Boeing
Often times without knowing
Facing despair
A blank stare
No emotion showing
Dark and gloomy inside, but outside I'm glowing
Focused on knowing what the future holds
Taking bold steps, no second guess on what I chose
When I fail, I win
I suppose
Because next time I know when to hold versus fold

Let Go

Loosen your grip for release
Relax your stride to walk away in peace
Free yourself from yesteryear
Clear your thoughts and be reborn again
Leave behind havoc and mayhem
Become your dreams and live them

The Tree

Walk with three legs
Listen with three ears
Smell with a second nose
Touch with a third hand
But don't speak
Let the silence reach you to teach
And therefore you shall reap the benefits of a seed
Planted for you to see a tree
Listen to the wind blow between its leaves
Watch it sway back and forth as it teases with ease
How can a tree communicate with me
How can I understand its purpose but I never heard it   speak
Silent but powerful is the tree

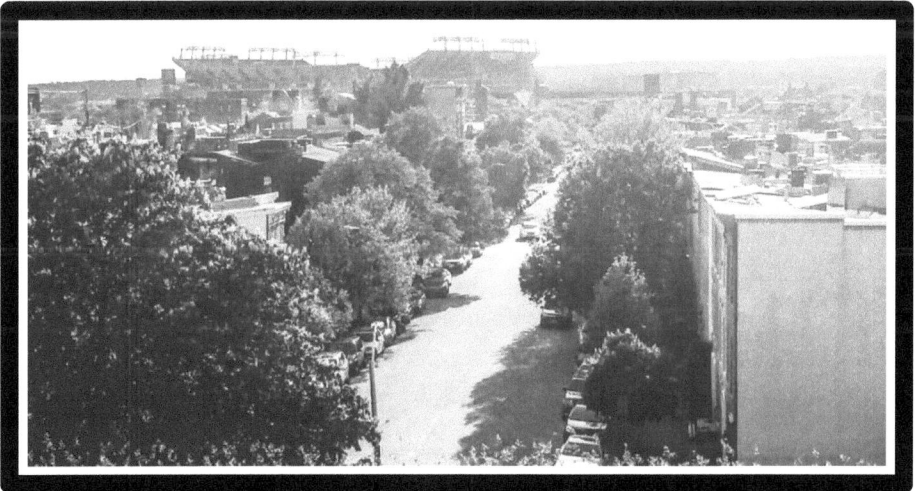

Opinions

Opinions are like socks
You wear them
Though they're hidden like in a box
Some shoes cover them
Never to reveal it's unorthodox
Though at day's end, those shoes come out of its lock
Some choose flip flops
Only revealing what's hot
Flaps cover the unorthodox
Needing correction like a crop
Some wear crocs
Careful not to reveal a lot
But when it's hot, there are no socks

Overseer

Overpower and destroy
Take what's not yours with force
And no remorse for the export
Of bodies from porches across the city
Armed with firearms, rather torches
In squad cars like on backs of horses
Who are these people who join these forces

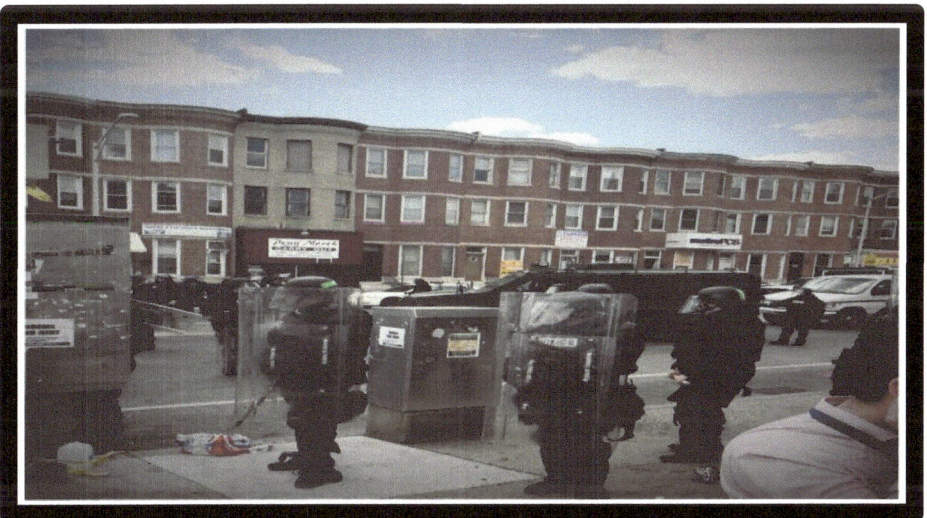

Untitled

If I don't succeed
Who will I be
Will I be invisible as folks pass me
Will my voice be acknowledged as fast as it's silenced
Will I be attacked with violence
Or biased opinion
Will my failure be highlighted
While achievements, not mentioned

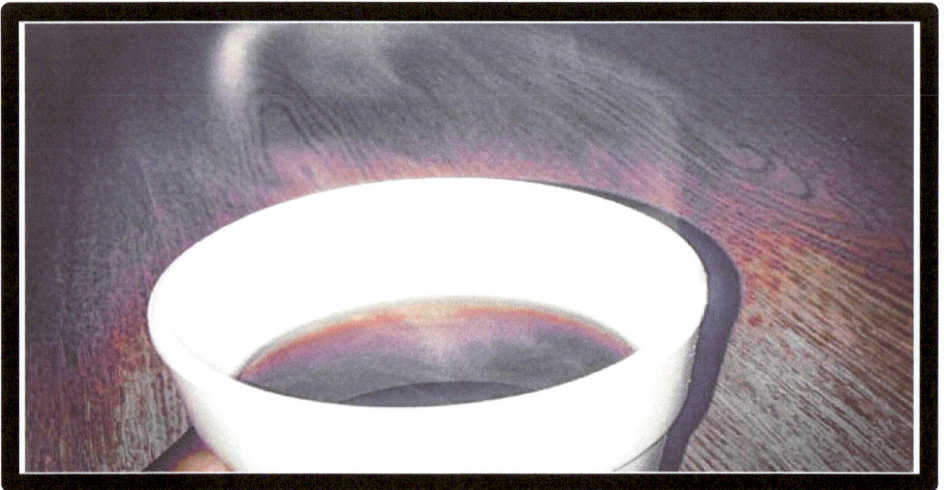

Age

Scare me never
The fright was clever but unmeasured
Tethered to tremors and shivering feathers
I'm better unfrightened but still nervous and a little unsettled
The dawn of a new battle is approaching
Whether I'm ready or not I'm hoping
Hoping that change keeps the focus on positivity
Those no longer here are living through me
Though they may have perished
They're a part of my legacy
Twenty nine years to breath, was I worthy
Or will I just casually turn thirty

Life Ain't Like Nickelodeon

I never saw Doug or Skeeter wearing wife beaters
Nor facing street corner thugs and leeches
I never saw Patti molested, nor Clarissa arrested
Or tested for sexual preferences
I never saw Kenan and Kel step over needles and shells
On the way to beat the bell
Real monsters with demons sleeping on bus stops in hell
I never saw cat dog shot in a house raid
I never saw Arnold robbed in a dice game
Who's to blame for those visions when there was no television
Who's testing these kids for PTSD instead of ADHD
Who's telling these kids that Nickelodeon is a false reality

Target

There's a new fix on the market
Its target is hardly of drinking age
Hardly departed from their parents place
Faced with the chase of euphoria
Torn between the fast life and conformity
Choosing a life of torture
Teachers yelling practice what I taught ya
Although those courses wouldn't prepare you for Baltimore front porches
Or stoops
Milk crates doubling as basketball hoops
And stools....
Never its intended use
Truth is, we weren't that ruthless as children
Although chilling
We witnessed murders and passed them over our feelings
Only to internalize the brain of our eyes
The visions that never gave a sentence
But surprise us when pain is revisited

The Watcher

I saw him, but he never saw me
What's he doing, why is he here
Is he falling toward destruction
I fear
I should probably steer clear if my fear is true to the tear
Gassed at the thought of self defense
Turning red from ear to ear
Should I follow and approach, even though I'm scared of those folks
These folks I greet with reproach
Keep your hands up high don't reach in your coat
I know there's a weapon close by
I know
These thugs shoot first and I won't
Become a statistic in a instant
He charged
Hand in his waistband
He's large
But wait
He's unarmed

He's Not Out

Hide it away
Water it down so it no longer has its taste
Change its shape, so that it switches in its place
Gone without a trace
His face no longer looks the same
The pain overshadowed his natural state
So plain, he'll never look again
Not quite beat out yet
But beat with stress without an outlet
Chest pain although his health aint gon south yet
He's still able to be made   stable
He's not outyet

Inclusion

How dare there be a multitude of ideas
Changing the culture and its reflection
Upset at it's changing complexion
Fetching outside the box for thoughts
Changing the direction

How dare you be offended when I speak
Those rotten words don't describe you
You're not like those others I see
I wouldn't lie toyou

Why do you care if I speak ill of those wild hoods
Just burn the city down
Give your kids a better childhood

How dare you have complaints
You should be happy to be here, you should feel safe
50 years ago you would've never walked in this place
So put a smile on your face
Before we find another one to take your place

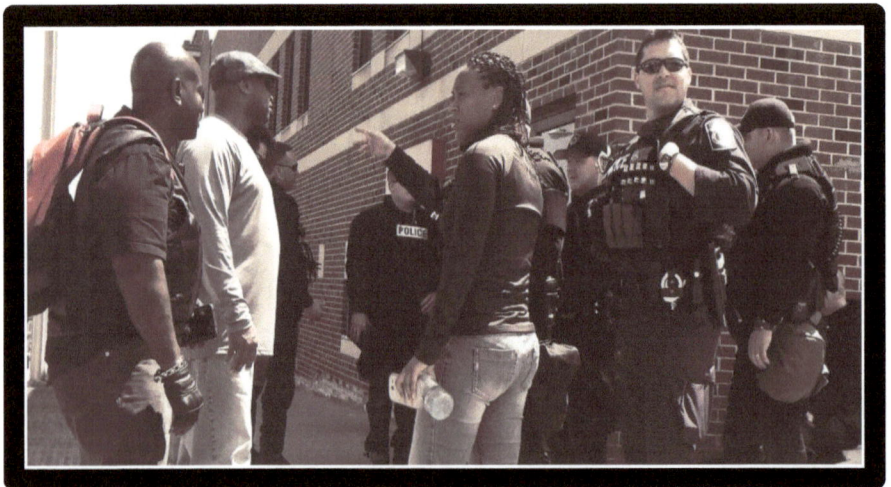

The Routine

Yesterday was the same as its predecessor
And the yester to that
Never festered a change
Or better yet, never changed a thing
Routinely we never change the things we do
The routine will kill you because it never changes you

Resistance

Withdrawal or pull back
The get away before facts are presented
A sentence given before a crime is committed
He fits the description with his cap that's fitted
Citizen resistance or passive aggressiveness
Defuse or agitate the present state
The residents decline your community occupation
You too would decline this torture they're faced with
But the denial of human suffering is amazing

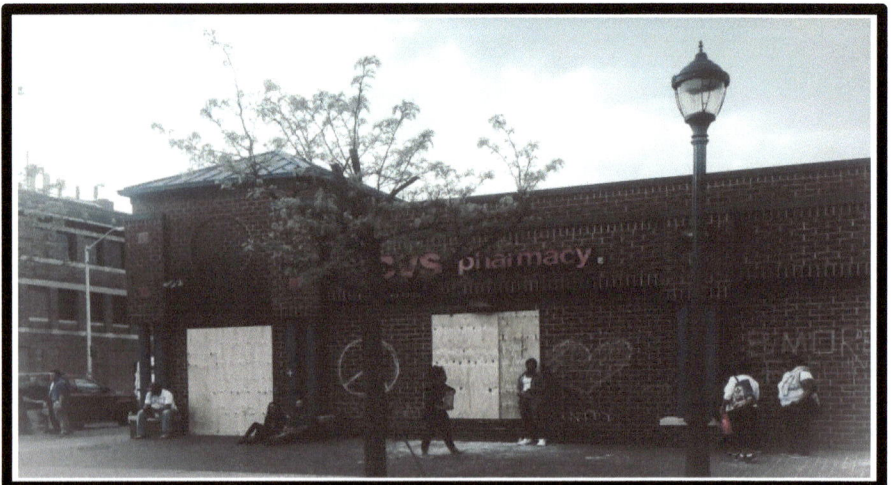

Not Her Too

She's had a rough day
Don't harm her for what she might say
It may bruise your ego, O.K.
Please just let her go
Go on her way

Let her see another day
Let her see her children play
Don't be alarmed at what she might say
Please don't shoot her
Please don't blow her away

Why is she a threat to you
Is it her afro, her brown skin
Or her strong attitude
Or reluctance to show gratitude
Please leave her alone
She's only a queen who's had it too

"The End"

Outro

Who are the ones who will carry the torch, bringing light to the youth left in darkness, haunted by constant death? Who will halt the constant fire on our neighborhoods? Who will protect our existence from violence? Change comes in many forms and can manifest in many ways as well. It can come in the form of cameras at the top of every street lamp to monitor your every action, or it can come in the form of legislation which actually makes the community safer. Change can scare someone so much, that one can be convinced that something is being taken from them. Physical change will never parallel mental change. Mental change is a delayed reaction to physical change, therefore conversation and therapy is needed. The poems you've just read are for therapeutic purposes.

The mind must be healed from the mental torture imposed on it by constant images of today's reality. The image of a neighbor lying dead in the street for hours can cause war-like post traumatic stress disorder. People carry that image with them to work, school, church; never stopping to reflect on one's own trauma. Urban living is fast and the grieving process may slow a person down. No one should carry that type of stress throughout life. No one should be led to the grave because life's overwhelming stress was too much for the heart to bear.

Therapy is the ultimate healer for rehabilitation. As the metaphors and similes flow, the mind is placed at ease, allowing thoughts to process without interruption or acknowledgement of the world around it. There is power in poetry and it creates an avenue for idle minds to navigate. The anger brewing on the avenues and streets can produce art in the form of rhyme and reason, drifting one away from the usual narratives of urban America.

Junist Harvey Jr.

NOTES

Alexander, M. (2012). *The New Jim Crow.* The Persus Books Group, LLC.
Rodrickks, D. (2015, May 23). Time For Leaders To Do The Right Thing For Baltimore's poorest Kids. *Baltimore Sun* .
Wise, T. (2015, May 5). The Crime of Innocence. *TimWise.org* .

Harvey Jr. Media, LLC.

www.ingramcontent.com/pod-product-compliance
Lightning Source LLC
LaVergne TN
LVHW010028070426
835513LV00001B/20